Secrets
Of
The Hunt

DAVID—

NEVER STOP "HUNTIN" THE TRUTH!

John 14:6

Chad Hampton
and
James Hampton

ISBN: 978-1-60383-055-3

Published by:
Holy Fire Publishing
Unit 116
1525-D Old Trolley Rd.
Summerville, SC 29485

www.ChristianPublish.com

Cover Design: Jay Cookingham

Printed in the United States of America and the United Kingdom

*IN MEMORY OF FELLOW HUNTER AND
FRIEND ROD BLUMERICH*

James would like to thank....

First and foremost my Heavenly Father for being faithful to me, even during the times when I took advantage of the cross and was not sold out to Him.

My mom and dad for leading us in the way we should go at such a young age. I love you.

My twin brother and best friend, Chad: Thank you for being a great example of a young man who is sold out and fully committed to Christ.

My wife Susan: Thank you for always being there for me and allowing me to pursue the purpose God has for my life.

My spiritual parents and mentors, Pastor Randy and Jane Hotchkiss.

The "Huntin the Truth" brothers: James Polly Jr., Al Ludwig, James Polly Sr., and special thanks to Paul Taylor. Thank you Paul for showing me what a true Christian brother really is.

Chad would like to thank...

My Lord, my everything, Jesus Christ, this book was your idea. May all glory be to You.

Mom and Dad, thank you for paving the way for us. I love you.

James, thank you for being the best brother and best friend a guy could have. I'm proud of you for who you are, and for following your dream.

My pastors, mentors, and friends, Pastor Randy and Jane Hotchkiss: True hunters of God.

Chad and James would like to thank...
Fellow hunter and friend, Joe Mitchell, thank you for your editing expertise on this project.

Donny Young. How could we forget about you?

TABLE OF CONTENTS

INTRODUCTON

It is the night before your 13th birthday. The next morning would be the first time in your life you would get the chance to deer hunt. The entire night you toss and turn waiting for your alarm to sound. Everything was ready. You have your clothes laid out on the floor, your broad heads sharpened, your bow in the case, and your backpack is packed. The anxiousness grows as you think back to the previous weekend when you and a friend set up your spot in an old fixed up stand on his property. You have the morning all planned out. You would sneak into the stand about thirty minutes before daylight, wait for first light, and shoot the first buck that comes within shooting range.

Finally, the alarm buzzes and you stand up in excitement. You put on your camo and take off for the woods. You arrive on time as planned and watch as creation begins to appear in the daylight. Visions of your first harvest dance through your head. You keep your eyes and ears open in anticipation of the first whitetail buck of the morning to step out into a shooting lane. Seconds of waiting turn into minutes, then into an hour, and then two. You look at your watch and it reads nine o'clock sharp. No sign of a deer. Confused, you begin to wonder why you haven't spotted a buck. It had been two hours! This was supposed to be easy right? Climb into your stand, wait for the deer to come, harvest a deer and then go home? You become frustrated. You climb out of your stand and head back.

What was going on? Why did you have such bad luck on your first hunt? It wasn't supposed to happen this way. It seemed like every other hunter you knew had deer within shooting range. The only living creatures you saw were squirrels and rabbits! Were you doing something wrong? Should you have done something different? Were there some secrets to harvesting whitetail deer?

How many of you reading this can relate to this story? If you have been hunting for any length of time you have been through this scenario. If I asked you the question, "What are some reasons you didn't see a deer" how would you respond? I assume that you would respond to me with questions of your own such as, "Was the area scouted?" or "Was the wind in my favor?" You might also ask me, "Did I wear cover scent?" or "Was my stand on a food source?" If I were sitting next to you right now we could probably exchange stories and secrets we have learned in our attempts to harvest our own trophy buck. Those are the ones we would call our own secrets of the hunt.

Maybe your life feels like this fictional scenario you just read about the first time you went hunting. You thought life was supposed to turn out different then it has. Maybe you're not happy with your life, and you're wondering if you're doing something wrong, or if there are secrets to harvesting happiness. Today we want to tell you stories and secrets we have learned in our attempts to hunt something much greater then a twelve point monster buck, something more majestic then a Boone and Crockett wall hanger, and something much more important then a spot on your local outdoor "Big Buck Night." We want to tell you secrets we've learned while hunting the truth about our lives: Gods purpose and plan for each of us. To find God's purpose for your life it is going to take the same passion, dedication, commitment, investigation, and faith it takes to harvest your big buck. This book will use the secrets of hunting whitetail to help you experience the harvest of knowing and living out God's unparalleled plan for your life. Are you ready to hunt?

Secret #1

Understanding Your Hunt
What Am I Really Hunting For?

Early afternoon rolls around and you figure you will go out and try your luck again! You slip on your clothes, spray on some cover scent, grab your back pack and bow, and head for the woods. You climb in your stand and sit down just in time to see a doe and small fawn step out of the woods across the bean field. Wow! You see deer already! This might not be so bad after all! Your heart begins to beat faster and you can feel the adrenaline start to move through your body. She's a nice size doe. You begin to wonder, "Should I shoot her?" You watch them as they cautiously make their way along the edge of the woods and toward you. You can hear your heart beating...thump thump...thump thump...thump thump. They get within shooting range and the doe walks to your right and stops right in the middle of your shooting lane! You have a decision to make. Do I shoot her, or do I wait for a buck? You figure you will try to stand up and make your decision. Just as you are about to stand up something catches your eye across they hayfield. You look up, and it's a buck! You put your binoculars to your eyes and count the points. It's a six point! It has an average size body and decent size horns, but it's a buck! You stand up to get a better look. He begins to move toward you on the same trail the doe and fawn came in. Your knees begin to shake, and buck fever is setting in! OH NO! You watch him as he moves down the trail and joins the doe and fawn on your shooting lane. The week before the season started you saw a monster buck roaming in your hayfield. Should you shoot this six point, or should you wait for a chance at the BIG ONE? It's a risky decision. Those monster bucks are smart, and there's a chance you may not see him all season! What should you do? You look at the six point and imagine his head and horns mounted on your living room wall. Still shaking you pull your bow up slowly and get ready to pull back. Just then something else catches your eye across the field. You keep your bow up and take a peak. IT'S HIM! It's the big one you saw before the season! You watch him graze. In the meantime the six point, doe, and fawn move on into *the woods and out of sight. You lower your bow and watch the monster. You pray that he comes down the same trail to your shooting lane. He begins to walk down your trail, and then he stops and walks in the opposite direction toward the downwind side of your stand. He walks straight downwind from you, puts his snout in the air, looks around for a minute, and heads back to where he came from and out of sight...NO! You had a chance at a nice doe and a six point but you waited for the big one and it backfired! Did you make the right decision?*

Every hunter reading this scenario has to make this decision every season. Whether the big one on your hunting land is an eight point, or a twenty point, most of us have chances to shoot decent size does or small bucks. Is that what we are really after though? Would you be satisfied to hunt your whole life for that big one and never get a chance to harvest him? Could you settle for a decent size doe or a small buck for your own personal record books? Let's face it, most of us have shot a doe or small buck and made the excuse,

"Well I shot it for the meat!" We can say that and fool everyone, but ourselves. We really shot it so we can at least say we harvested something! Whether you admit it or not, there is a deep longing in the heart of a true hunter to bag that big one, and a true hunter with that kind of passion will pass up many does and small bucks and not stop until he experiences the harvest of the monster on his hunting land!

Just as there is a deep passion to bag that big buck, whether we admit it or not, God has put the longing in the heart of every human to experience the "big one" in your hunt for God and the truth about your life. Isn't there more to life then this? What is the truth about our lives? The real truth is no matter what has happened in your life, or no matter what satan or any person says about you God's purpose and plan for you is bigger then you even realize! No matter how many mistakes you've made, or even if your life seems hopeless at this moment, God still has a purpose and plan for your life. What is the "big one" on this hunt?

It's the full potential of what God has had planned for your life from the very beginning. Jeremiah 1:5 in the Message Bible it says, *"Before I shaped you in the womb, I knew all about you. Before you saw the light of day, I had holy plans for you..."* God had this purpose and plan before you were even thought of by your earthly parents, and it's a plan that is more then you could ever imagine! Ephesians 3:20 in the Message Bible says, *"God can do anything you know-far more than you could ever imagine or guess or request in your wildest dreams!"* It is also a plan God has designed to make you truly happy and fulfilled. Jeremiah 29:11 in the Message Bible says, *"I know what I am doing. I have it all planned out-plans to take care of you, not abandon you, plans to give you the future you hope for."* God has a plan for your life. He knows what He's doing and He wants to teach you how you can experience the "big buck" He has planned for you. Do you want to bag the big one? Are you satisfied with just living and experiencing some or most of what God has for you?

Are you satisfied with the "does" and "small bucks" in life? Or do you want to bag the MONSTER? Are you truly happy and fulfilled? Come along with us as we go on a hunt for God and the truth about your life.

The Love and the Glimpse

You stroll in from your evening hunt disappointed because you didn't get a chance at the big buck. You open the door to your house, begin to take your clothes off, put them in your plastic bin and put the cover on to prevent any unusual odor from getting on your clothes for your next hunt. You walk to the kitchen and notice you have a message on your machine. You push the button and listen to your best friend ask you if you'd like to go with him to his hunting land in the northern part of the state. You remember him telling you a month before that there were rumors that the biggest buck in the state was living in those parts! Your eyes light up. Let's do it! You pick up the phone and call your friend back to accept the invitation. He informs you that you will be leaving in three hours and staying for two weeks. You quickly pack your bags and gear and head north.

The ride north seems just a few minutes long because of the anticipation of what you hope to see. You pull into the driveway that leads back to camp and head back to the cabin.

You enter the woods and drive for a mile. You pull up to the cabin and get out stretching from the ride. You start to walk around the back of the cabin and see a big open field. You stop to take a long hard look. You see the wind blowing the leaves off the trees, the sun setting over the horizon, and small game roaming the field. Ah, what a sight to behold. Hunting season! Your buddy starts to tell you about the record book buck that they saw twice last year, but never got a shot at him. He tells you that this buck is the smartest buck around, and has been sneaking around his camp for years. As your listening to your friend talk about his massive buck, you see a deer appear in the back corner of the field. You pull your binoculars from the truck and take a look...THERE HE IS! It's almost like he knew you were coming and he wanted to tease you and give you a glimpse of him. You watch him walk down the edge of the field and he stops and looks at you, shakes his head a bit like he is acknowledging you are there, and then slowly walks into the woods at the other end of the field. You feel challenged, you feel ready. You whisper under your breath, "Your mine buddy."

What is it that keeps you motivated to get up so early every morning to go out and have a chance to harvest your deer? My brother and I often laugh because if we knew we should get up at five in the morning to go to work and get a little extra overtime in we would roll over and push the snooze button and sleep in until the last minute. It's not that way with hunting! We are usually up early and waiting to head to the woods! What is it that makes a man go to the extremes to bag that big buck? We believe its two things. First is the love of hunting. There is something about the challenge of trying to study and harvest a smart buck. The second is that glimpse of that big buck you've seen on T.V or on a real hunt that you pray to have a chance at harvesting. These two are what keep you motivated. We believe these two things are the same thing that will keep you motivated to continue to hunt God, His truth, and His plan for your life. Before we go any further we would like to tell you the ultimate motivation for our hunt for God. It's our love for Him! Since the day we found out how much God really loves us, it has motivated us to seek Him and His plan for our lives. We strive to live out that plan. How much does He love us, and how much does He love you? The Bible says in John 3:16 that *"For God so loved the world that He gave his only begotten Son, that whoever believes in him should not perish but have everlasting life."* God loved us so much that He sent His Son Jesus, which is God made flesh, to come to earth to die for our sins on the cross so we can be free of sin. Because of His great sacrifice we can begin to find His plan for our lives, and be with Him in Heaven one day. If you really meditate on His sacrifice and plan it will cause you to love Him more and want to seek God and His plan for you.

If you study the Bible you will see that not only does God's love for a person motivate them to seek Him, but you will also a glimpse of His plan for each and every one of us. In Matthew 16, Jesus is talking to His disciples about who they thought He really was. Peter answered correctly in verse 16 and said, *"You are the Christ, the son of the living God."* Then Jesus gave Peter a glimpse of his "big buck." Jesus said in verse 18, *"And I also say to you that you are Peter; and on this rock I will build My church..."* WOW! That's one big buck! Jesus told Peter that He was a rock, a foundation, and Jesus said He would build His church on Peter. Now that's a glimpse! Notice He didn't tell Peter how He would do that. Jesus gave Peter just enough information to stay motivated to keep seeking Him for answers on how He would use Peter as the foundation of His church.

God has the same plan for you. Does this mean that I am saying that God's plan for you is as big as God's plan for Peter? Yes! Your life is just as important to what God wants to get done in this world as Peter's life. As you go on this hunt, let the love you have for God, and that glimpse of God's great plan for your life keep you motivated to keep hunting God and His plan for you. If you have not started a relationship with God and asked Him to forgive you of your sins and live in your heart the Bible says that you can do it right now and begin your hunt! Romans chapter 10:9-10 says, *"That if you confess with your mouth the Lord Jesus and believe in your heart that God has raised him from the dead, you will be saved. For with the heart one believes unto righteousness, and with the mouth confession is made unto salvation."*

Ask Him right now to forgive you of your sins and become Lord of your life, and then come with us as we begin teach you the secrets of harvesting truth as you hunt Him.

Secret #2

You have to scout your area and set up your stand!

You can't believe what you just saw. You just saw the big one! You look at your friend and he looks back at you, and you're both speechless. A smile appears on both of your faces at the same time. You already know what the other is thinking. There is still a great deal of daylight left, so you decide to take a walk back to the woods and begin to scout your area and find your spot to hunt. You grab your backpack and head for the woods. As you walk through the field you notice some pretty well traveled trails that lead to the north end of the woods. You follow the trails and see that the woods is connected to a bean field, an open field with a pond in the middle, and another field that has a few rows of pine trees. Perfect! There is a food source, a water source, and cover. As you walk along the edges of these fields you begin to see sign that the deer have been around. You see some fresh deer droppings along the trail, and you walk a little further and see some beds in the weeds where the deer have been sleeping. You also notice some very heavily used trails going back and forth from the fields. You stop to take in the information and put together a strategy of where you think the deer are coming from and where would be the best place to set up your stand. Just then you look to the left, and you see a buck scrape on the ground underneath a hanging branch of a tree. You walk over to check out the scrape and see its pretty fresh and pretty well dug up! You look to the right and see a huge buck rub on a large tree. Wow! By the looks of the rub you are sure it must be from the big one. You figure this is where he must be hanging out, and why wouldn't he? This spot has everything. It has food, water, cover, and there is sign of does walking around this area. The perfect combination! You walk along the edge of the woods and find a good tree that will allow you to use your climbing stand. You find a good straight tree downwind of the main trails, rubs, and scrapes you scouted, and you climb up the tree cutting down branches along the way. You finally get up to about fifteen feet and turn around to check out your *area. It's a perfect spot. You climb down your tree excited about your spot and head for the cabin.*

How many times have you gone hunting on a whim and gone out to the field, picked a spot as you went and sat down and harvested a big buck without any investigation of your area? Unless you get lucky often, then I'm sure your answer to that question is almost never. If you're a serious hunter and you're reading this then I'm sure you already know how important it is to scout your area to see the activity of the does and bucks before you pick your spot. We all know that deer hang around food sources like crop fields and acorns, and they hang around places with water like ponds, streams and rivers. We know the sign that deer have been around. There are the footprints, the droppings, the trails, the scrapes and rubs, or even the sound of a deer blowing at you along the way when they get a smell of you. I HATE THAT! We also know that deer like to be close to cover like thickets and pine trees so they can rest in peace, and that they have very good smell, which makes it important to sit downwind of where they will most likely appear. Scouting your area and positioning yourself in the most likely spot for deer to pass through is crucial to bagging that big buck.

Just as scouting and positioning yourself to bag the big one on your hunt is important, it's also just as important on your hunt for God and His plan for your life. The second secret to getting a harvest on your hunt for God is to scout out and pick an area where you can get away from distractions, be still, and listen to what God impresses on your heart everyday. Scouting out a place where you can position yourself for your hunt for God, means to hear Gods voice. This is crucial to knowing Gods truth and plan for your life. Remember, God knows the plan He has for us, and for us to know that He has to tell us that plan, which comes from hearing His voice. God speaks to all of us in many different ways, but if we aren't still and focused we won't hear His voice just as if we aren't still and focused we wont let that big buck get close enough to us to harvest it! How many times have you just grabbed your bow and trampled through the woods at a steady pace and bagged a buck? Never! Doing that makes way too much noise to be able to harvest your trophy. It's the same with God. If we will just take some time sitting still and positioning ourselves in a comfortable quiet place where we are surrounded with good "sign" to be able to hear God you will hear Him! Oh, how hard it is for us men and women to do that for God, and yet easy it is for us to do while hunting! Just as we know where deer like to hang out because of the sign, we also know the places that are quiet. Those are the places you will get a harvest and hear God most clearly just like quiet places gives us a better chance to harvest our buck. Those places aren't where kids are running around and screaming or the T.V is blaring! So, is the best spot to hear God sitting in your office chair as you're trying to work? No! Commotion at work is not good sign. There is too much going on to try to focus on God. Is the best spot to hear God sitting at the kitchen table trying to eat breakfast and rush out the door to work? No! Rush...rush...rush...is not good sign! Is the best spot to hear God sitting in your recliner while your reading the daily newspaper? No! God wants us to be still and focus on HIM alone!

In 1 Kings Chapter 19:11 God told Elijah to go and stand on the mountain so He could speak to him. *"Then He said, 'Go out, and stand on the mountain before the Lord.' And behold, the Lord passed by, and a great and strong wind tore into the mountains and broke the rocks in pieces before the Lord, but the Lord was not in the wind; and after the wind came an earthquake, but the Lord was not in the earthquake; and after the earthquake a fire, but the Lord was not in the fire; and after the fire a still small voice."* This voice was from God, and just as these verses tell us, we will not hear Gods voice the best when things around us are distracting, but only when it's quiet and calm because Gods voice is still and small and it takes effort to hear Him. I'm not saying God won't speak to you at any time. God is always speaking to us, we just aren't always listening, and it's easier to listen when we are still. Psalms 46:10 says, *"Be still and know that I am God..."*

Whether it's for 10 minutes or an hour, being still and listening to God's still small voice in your scouted area will increase your chances of getting a harvest on your hunt for God and His plan for your life!

Now that you have picked out an area that will best position you to get a harvest, its time to pick the tree and set up the stand! You can have a great spot, but if you don't find a place where you can be still, listen and look for the deer coming, and be able to watch what's going on it will decrease your chances to harvest your deer. Just as this is important to your deer hunt, it's just as important on your God hunt. Picking a spot to set your stand up so you can sit, look, watch, and listen is just like your prayer time with God. You've picked a spot away from distractions, you sit down and begin to look, watch, and listen for God voice, and that starts through prayer and meditation. Most people think prayer is just something you do when you want to ask God for something or want something from Him. Although that is a part of prayer, we have found as we study the Bible and pray that prayer is just as much or more about focusing on God, meditating, and listening to Him. Prayer is a time where you can ask forgiveness and give all your burdens to God, tell Him your feelings, ask Him questions, ask for direction, and then prayer is just as much listening to what God has to say back to you through meditation on Him. God wants to speak to you, but remember, His voice is usually still and small, so we have to listen carefully. So scout out your area, find a good spot with the sign around that is still and calm, and position yourself to hear Gods still small voice everyday. Then, position yourself to hear what God's harvest is for your life.

Secret #3

Having your weapon and sighting it in is crucial to your harvest.

With the thoughts of the big buck and the sign of him that you just saw dancing in your head, you open the back of your SUV and begin to take your gear into camp and get set for the night. After you take your clothes and gear in you go back out to grab your bow and target. There are still a few hours of light left and you remember that your bow has been shooting a little low and to the right, so you decide to do some last minute practicing for the morning hunt and make sure your bow is sighted in. You put your arrow on the rest, pull back and aim...THUD! Your arrow hits the target a little low and to the right just like you thought. You adjust your sights slightly, and put another arrow on. You pull back to shoot again...THUD! Still a little right, but the height is right on. You adjust your sights one more time and put another arrow on your rest and pull back...THUD! It is a direct hit in the center of the target. You smirk and play in your mind your arrow hitting the big one through the center *of the heart and watching him drop after running fifty yards. You look over your bow one last time to check to see if everything is in place and put the bow back in the case. Everything is ready to go. The area is scouted, stand is put up, and your weapon is ready. Watch out big buck!*

I know everyone of you reading this knows the feelings and emotions you experience when you get to this point. You have waited all year to get to this moment. The hunt is about to begin. I want you to stop for a minute and consider a couple of things before we move on. Imagine a hunt without a weapon! Right now you are probably saying, "WHAT? Go hunting without a weapon? There is no reason to hunt unless you have a weapon to harvest the animal!" You're exactly right, and not only is that principle true on your hunt for your deer, but it is also true on your hunt for the truth. If you don't have your weapon you can't harvest the truth.

What is the weapon we use on our hunt for the truth about what God has for our lives? Our weapon is the Bible! If we are hunting for the truth about our lives, then we must research and know the One who created us and knows the truth about us. In God's Word it tells us that the Bible is God's words to us to tell us the truth about our lives! 2 Timothy 3:16-17 says, *"All scripture is given by inspiration of God, and is profitable for doctrine, for reproof, for correction, for instruction in righteousness, that man may be complete, thoroughly equipped for every good work."* This verse tells us that God gives us everything we need to have a complete or successful hunt in His Word.

The Bible even mentions itself as a type of weapon that goes deep into the center of our heart! In Hebrews 4:12 it says, *"For the Word of God is living and powerful, and sharper then any two-edged sword, piercing even to the division of soul and spirit, and of joints and marrow, and is a discerner of the thoughts and intents of the heart."* This means that Gods word, the Bible, goes deep into our hearts to show us our real thoughts and intentions, and shows us what God's thoughts and intentions and truth is for our lives! WOW! We really do have the perfect weapon to have a successful hunt!

Ok, now we know that we can't harvest our deer without a weapon. Now I want you to think about something else. If you had a weapon, but never sighted it in, would it be likely that you would harvest your animal? Probably not, unless you have a lucky shot! Practicing with your weapon and sighting it in, or becoming accurate with it is just as important as having the weapon itself. Practicing, or reading, memorizing and meditating in Gods word will make you accurate on your hunt for the truth about your life and give you a great chance for a harvest! Joshua 1:8 tells us this principle. It says, *"This Book of the Law shall not depart from your mouth, but you shall meditate in it day and night, that you may observe to do according to all that is written in it. For then you will make your way prosperous, and then you will have good success."* This verse tells us that if we know and meditate on God's word and become accurate with it we will be prosperous and have good success on our hunt! It is impossible to know the truth about our lives unless we know where to find that truth and to be accurate in knowing what that truth is! I love The Message Bible translation of 2 Timothy 3:16-17. It says, *"The Bible tells us who we are and shows us what God has shaped us to do..."* How can you live out God's full plan for your life unless you know that? Get your weapon out of the case and begin to sight it in! It's almost time for opening morning!

Secret #4

Getting up early

The alarm clock buzzes, and it's time to get up. All night long you were so excited with anticipation that it doesn't seem like you slept a wink. You decide you'll just sleep a few more minutes because you are so tired. You reach over and turn your alarm off. You fall back into a half sleep and when you open your eyes you think only fifteen minutes have passed. You turn over and look at the clock. OH NO! Ninety minutes have passed! You look out the window and it's already daylight! You jump up and put your gear on, yell at your friend to get up, grab your backpack and head for your stand. You walk fast and start to sweat as you get to the edge of the woods and your stand comes into sight. You stop to take a look around for deer. You look across the field that your stand is on. There are no deer in sight. As you glance back toward your stand some horns catch your eye about 50 yards from your stand. It's an eight point buck! He catches sight of you and runs off into the woods. You missed a chance at a buck because you weren't out there on time! It's not the monster, but it sure was a nice buck! Disappointed, you head to your stand and sit down with hopes that another one will show.

Boy, how many times has this happened, huh? I think at one time or another we have all had a lazy morning when we wanted to sleep in just a few more minutes and it came back to haunt us! If you've been hunting any amount of time you know when the deer move most often, early in the morning and late in the evening. We know as hunters we should be out there a little before daylight to let things settle down, and stay until hunting hours are over for our best chance to harvest our monster. That means getting up early, and sometimes staying late! There's no written hunting law that you have to get up early and be ready for your best chance to bag your buck, but we all know that when we do we have a better chance of a harvest. Its better then sitting out during mid-day hours when you rarely see a thing besides some small game and the shadows of the trees as the sun comes up and goes back down! Plus, how many hunters can just sit out in their stand all day everyday, unless you're on a hunting vacation! We've got things to do during the day!

Much of the hunting literature that is out there suggests hunting whitetail in the morning rather then in the evening. Even though we don't totally agree with that suggestion, and even though you don't have to, it is a good idea to get up and get in your stand early to have your best chance at bagging the big one.

Just as this principle applies to harvesting your big one, we believe it also applies to your hunt for God and His plan for your life. God wants to speak to you, fill you up with His Spirit, and get you ready to fulfill His plan for your upcoming day. Just as you could miss your chance at the big one if you're not up early and ready, you could miss some important truth that God has for your life for that day or your future. Maybe He wants to encourage you, warn you, give you direction, give you an idea or give you wisdom for the day, or maybe He just wants you to spend time in His presence communing with him. Psalms 63:1 says, "O God, thou art my God; Early I will seek You; My soul thirsts for You; My flesh longs for You in a dry and thirsty land where there is no water." If you have the true hunter's passion, sometimes we feel this way about wanting to bag that big buck. Everything in us wants to put him on a mount on our wall. God wants us to have that same desire and passion for Him. God called David a man after His own heart. David lived out Gods true plan for his life, and tells us here that he got up early on his hunt for God. In fact, in Psalms David mentions that he prayed three times a day. He prayed in the morning, at the noontime, and at night! Now that's hunting all day!

It's tough to get up in the morning. No one likes it. Everyone wants to just sleep a few more minutes, but just like on your hunt for your buck getting up early and being consistent will pay off eventually.

Jesus showed us this principle. In Mark 1:35 it says, *"Now in the morning, having risen a long while before daylight, He went out and departed to a solitary place; and there He prayed."* Jesus knew how important it was to get up early and spend time with His Father to start out the day, and if you study the Gospels you will see He also took small amounts of time during the day to pray and seek His Father.

Secret #5

Put in your time!

You look out over the field and it begins to fade into the darkness. It's time to head in. You tie your string to your bow and lower it carefully and climb down your tree. No sign of deer. You meet your friend at the cabin and tell him your story of how you kicked up the eight point on the way out because you were late. He tells you he didn't see a deer all day long. You grab a bite to eat and a soda and hope that tomorrow will bring a harvest. There are thirteen days to go.

For the next week you are up early and in late. You see a few does, but no bucks. What's going on? Your in a good spot, you saw sign that they are around, you even saw a big buck your first time out, so you know they are out there, but you haven't seen any bucks. Three more days pass by and you see no bucks, only more does and a couple button bucks. Two more days left. You are starting to get antsy. You think about moving your stand to another location, but you've put so much time in here, and you know this is a great spot. You think maybe they are moving in the mid-day hours when you come in for lunch, so the next day you pack a lunch and decide to sit all day long.

This is one thing about hunting that ISN'T a secret. More times then not you go to the stand and either don't see any deer at all or don't see the buck that you want to harvest. Harvesting a buck takes time and effort. It takes even more time and effort to harvest a wall hanger. Even though there is nothing more peaceful then to sit out in God's creation and enjoy it for hours, most of us don't have or want to put in the time it takes to bag a whitetail buck, let alone the big one. So, that leaves us two choices. We put in the time and effort, or we don't. But, the secret is, the more time and effort you put into it the better chance you will have to harvest your monster. Once again, just as this principle applies to hunting deer, it also applies to your hunt for God and His plan for your life. It comes down to one question. How bad do you want to bag the big one? If you want it bad enough then putting in the time necessary is essential! It might mean going out early in the morning, going back out in the afternoon early and staying until dark, or it might even mean making the sacrifice to stay out all day during the rut!

Just as there are times when we don't see a deer for many hunts, sometimes there are times where God will withhold our harvest from us for a purpose. Don't you think that the most exciting part of the hunt is the search, the wait, the anticipation, and even the challenge of outsmarting and waiting out a big buck? Well, in a way it's the same way on our hunt for God. Sometimes God withholds truth, wisdom, and direction from us so that we will continue to seek Him for it. If God told us everything about the truth and plan He has for our lives we wouldn't need to lean on Him to know what's next and we would just live it out! God wants us to be dependent on Him for everything, which is why God reveals truth about your life to you in a sporadic way. Sometimes even making you wait in His presence or seek Him for many "hunts" before you start to get a harvest, get some direction and wisdom, and have God move in your life. He's designed it that way so we will continue to hunt Him daily.

In our hunt for God and His plan for our lives there is one thing we need to be reminded of from time to time. God doesn't want us to focus on the harvest we can get from Him, but to focus just on knowing and loving Him more and growing closer in your relationship with Him, and the harvest will come. If we just focus on hunting God alone and not the harvest, then the harvest will happen naturally. We can become so focused on the hunt that we forget why we are hunting in the first place. We are hunting God because we love Him for what He did for us on the cross, and not for what He can give us or do for us. Keep that in mind.

Jeremiah 29:13 says, *"And you will seek Me and find Me, when you search for me with all your heart."* The words seek and hunt have similar definitions. If we hunt our monster with all of our heart and do the things necessary to bag him we will harvest him eventually, and God tells us here that if we hunt him with all of our hearts we will find Him and His plan for our lives. Get up early, hunt with all of your heart, put the necessary time in because you want to know and love God more, and you will find God.

Secret #6

Battling the Elements

You grab your lunch and put it in your backpack. It's going to be an all day hunt. You grab your bow and head for the stand. You climb into your stand, pull your bow up, and get settled. It's a cool crisp morning with a steady cool breeze. You watch as nature begins to appear in the daylight. You're hoping this could be the morning of the big harvest. As you glance over your field you feel a cold breeze blow across your face and the wind begins to pick up drastically. You look off to the north and you see some darks clouds form in the distance. A storm is brewing. The sky gets darker as the clouds approach. You hear and smell the rain coming. Blah! You didn't hear of any rain in the forecast. You don't have your rain gear. It starts to sprinkle. You know with the rain you won't be able to hear the deer coming, so you watch intently for any movement. It starts to rain harder, but not bad enough to make you want to head for the cabin. The wind blows even harder now and your

51

tree begins to sway back and forth. You tighten your safety belt and continue to watch. After a while it starts to pour, and you wonder if you should just get down and go home. Besides, how many deer are you going to see in this wind and rain, and even if you do get a shot how would you track the deer with the rain washing away the blood? Minutes turn into an hour and it still doesn't stop raining. You start to get distracted and irritated at the wind and rain. You feel the water soak through your coat and the wind begins to make you cold. You start to shake. "Is this really worth it?" you think. You begin to get upset. Only two weeks here, and only two days left to hunt and it has to rain! You get up, tie your bow to the string and climb down your tree and head for home. You get inside and get settled in for lunch. You notice your friend never came in, so you figure he must have waited out the storm. A couple hours later you see him walk in the door and he has a big grin on his face. "Did you get him?" you ask. "No" he answers. "But about 10 minutes after you got down and came home I watched a nice buck walk right underneath your stand!" OH NO! If you *just would have waited it out! If you wouldn't have gotten frustrated and distracted you could have bagged a big one! You put your hands over your face in disappointment. "What was I thinking?"*

I hate the elements. I wish that every hunt would be cold enough to keep the mosquitoes away, but sunny and warm enough to just wear light hunting clothes. Living in Michigan that's impossible! I hate hunting in rain, snow, high winds, and arctic like temperatures that Michigan brings every deer season. The elements are frustrating, inconvenient, uncomfortable, and most of all distracting! It disturbs everything. Rain stops the crispy sound of the deer walking on the fallen leaves toward you and washes the blood away when you hit a deer. High winds make you feel like your tree is going to fall over with you attached to it! If there is snow that means its cold and you have many layers of clothes on that just make it hard to get in your stand and maneuver for a shot. No matter how many pairs of socks you have on your toes freeze! In the end every one of the elements distracts you from every part of harvesting your deer. The sit, the wait, using your weapon, and finding and harvesting the deer are affected. Even in warmer weather it can ruin a hunt for a wounded deer because it can spoil the deer before you can find it! Why can't everything be perfect?

Sometimes I find myself on my hunt for God battling life's elements and asking the same questions! Why can't everything just be perfect? Hunting God would be so much easier! There are so many distracting elements you face in your life while hunting for God. There are high winds, all kind of storms, and cold times in life that distract you from hunting God and spending time with Him. People hurt you, mistakes bother you, bills are late, kids need to be fed, and work stinks. On and on the "storms" come and go distracting you from your hunt. There are times where you might just want to get out of your stand and head home and just go to sleep because of the elements. You thought hunting and spending time with Him was suppose to be a chance to get away from it all, but the storms linger in your mind as you hunt God and try to spend time in His presence.

Just as we can't stop the elements of the weather from passing through our area, God tells us that the storms of life will also come our way when we are hunting Him, and He brings or allows those storms for a reason. In the book of James, Chapter 1:2-4 the Bible says, *"My brethren, count it all joy, when you fall into various trials, knowing that the testing of your faith produces patience. But let patience have its perfect work, that you may be perfect and complete, lacking nothing."* Many times, satan will bring these storms in our lives to distract us from hunting God, and sometimes we bring the distracting storms on ourselves, but either way God will never give us more then we can handle, and He allows these storms for a reason. God brings or allows the storms in our lives to perfect our faith, and produce the patience we need to harvest our monster.

The more we endure the storms in life the more patience we will have to endure through anything that is thrown at us, and patience will help us stay focused on getting our harvest!

God doesn't bring or allow these storms in our lives to distract us, we distract ourselves and focus on the storms and elements rather then God. If we focus more on the storms and elements and give up and go home we might miss our chance at the big one!

Secret #7

Taking Risks

It's the last day. Your alarm goes off, and you shut it off and say a quick prayer. For the last time, on this hunt for the record book buck, you grab your gear and weapon and head for your stand. You climb in your stand and sit down. It's the perfect morning, cool and crisp with no wind. You're unusually tired on this morning, so you tighten up your safety belt and begin to doze off while trying to keep your eyes open. You're startled and awakened by a couple of squirrels chasing each other. As you doze off again a large bird unnoticeably lands on the branch next to you, makes a loud noise and wakes you again. You open your eyes and standing about a hundred yards off is a doe walking in front of you coming from the opposite corner of the field. Two more does come from the same spot and hang out down in that corner, then two more. You spot a small buck that comes from behind you out in the field and he heads for the corner. You've seen many deer hanging out in this corner the past two weeks. *You wonder if that corner is the hot spot! If the doe go there then it is most likely that us where the monster will show up. You sit the rest of the morning and into the afternoon. You begin to get hungry. The thought of moving your stand into the corner where all the action is crosses your mind over and over. "Should I?" you wonder. It's a big risk, but there is only one more hunt and it's time to go home. Maybe it might be best just to wait it out here. You've had a few in shooting range. You have a decision to make. As your contemplating your next move, some movement catches your eye from the opposite side of the filed, coming from the high weeds. IT'S HIM! It's the monster you saw pulling into the camp on the first day. He walks into the field. The other deer see him and stop what they are doing. He stops and puts his nose in the air to take a quick smell, takes a look around, and then starts to walk across the field in front of you. He gets about seventy-five yards away and he's moving at a steady pace. You put your grunt call to your mouth and grunt twice. He stops and looks your way. You begin to breath deep and hard shaking all over. He looks your way again, and then looks toward the corner keeping an eye on the does. He begins to walk toward the other deer, so you hit your grunt call one more time to stop him. He pays no attention. You watch him as he walks to the corner and begins to chase a doe. You watch as the monster and doe run out of sight, then the rest of the deer with them. You decide you are going to move your stand to the corner. It's a huge risk, but you know you might have to take big risks to bag the big one. The corner seems like the hot spot and the forecast calls for wind that will be going right from your stand to the corner. Now would be a good time to move. You climb down from your tree and go to the corner and pick out a tree for the evening hunt. Will your risk pay off?*

There is one aspect of hunting that I completely overlooked for many years that is essential to harvesting the biggest of bucks: Taking risks! I was always so scared to take a risk because I thought I would fail and miss my chance at the big one if I did. Even though all the information around me and the sign that I saw pointed in the direction of changing something and taking a risk, I always chose not to do something different out of fear. Think about the situation above. Would you take a risk and move your stand, or would you stay put? I can say now that I have taken many risks to bag the big one, but does it always pay off? Not every time, but most times it does if the sign and research seem to point to it. The times it paid off there was a great harvest and I never would have experienced that harvest unless I took the risk. One key thing I try to live by when taking a risk is the pattern I see in the deer and my gut feeling about it. More times then not it pays off.

Taking risks was not only an element of my hunt for my monster buck that I had overlooked, but also on my hunt for God and the full potential of His plan for my life. If I want to experience all that God has planned for me from the beginning then I have to take a risk. Now I'm sure some of you reading this are saying, "But taking risks in life is scary! It's uncomfortable and I'm comfortable right where I'm at!" Yes, it is more secure to be comfortable, but just as in hunting, you will never know what kind of harvest you will get unless you take some risks in life. Also as in hunting, I take risks in life based on two things. The first is the patterns of other people in the Bible who took risks, and the feeling I get down in my gut when I know God is leading me to take a risk.

As you start becoming accurate with your weapon, reading your Bible, you will begin to notice patterns of your harvest. You will start to read and learn about others in the Bible who are on the same hunt you are on, and you will learn patterns all of the these people shared that led them to harvest there big one! One of the patterns that all of the people who lived out Gods full plan for their lives is God asked each one of them to take risks to harvest the big one, and when they obeyed they eventually got a great harvest!

Take a look at Abraham. In Genesis 12 God asked Abraham to take a risk and leave his home to a place that God would show him as he went. GOD NEVER TOLD HIM WHERE! Now that's a risk, and how uncomfortable would that be? But Abraham obeyed and took the risk, and he got a huge harvest and God blessed him greatly. Take a look at Noah. In the times of Noah it had never rained, the earth was watered from the ground up, and he lived a great distance from any major body of water. God told Noah to build an Ark that would save him and his family from a flood God would bring that would wipe out everything on earth. How goofy did that look to other people? It had never rained and there was no water nearby, and Noah spent 120 years building the ark! He must be crazy right? Noah took a risk and obeyed God, and he got a harvest. Noah, his family, and at least two of every kind of animal were saved after the flood.

The Bible is full of stories of men and women who took risks and went to extremes to obey God. Obedience to God and taking risks to obey Him is essential if you want to harvest Gods monster plan for your life. When God asks you to take a risk, take the risk and obey Him no matter how uncomfortable it is. You'll be glad you did!

SECRET # 8

FIRING YOUR WEAPON-OBEDIENCE

All afternoon you've been packing up your things and loading them in the truck for the ride home. You take your last bag and pack it in the truck leaving out your hunting gear and weapon. It's time for the last hunt. You grab your things and head for your new spot in the corner of the field. You climb up your tree and sit down and begin to scan out your new area. There is more sign here then you thought! As you scan the areas you see fresh scrapes and rubs and some heavily used trails. As you sit you begin to think back on the hunting season up to this point. You think about how well you scouted your area, about how much time you've spent out in your spot, the different weather and storms you've dealt with on your hunts, and about the mistakes you've made and learned from. A few minutes pass by, and then an hour. You think about going home after this hunt, and you become sad. Just then something catches your eye. It's a doe coming across the field. You watch her stop and eat, and then she walks right underneath your stand. A few minutes later you see a doe shoot out from the woods being chased by a small buck and they run to you and stop. Your blood starts pumping hard and your adrenaline races through your body. You hear a deer walking up behind you. You look back. It's another buck, an eight point! You start to think you've made the right move by switching spots. Deer are running all around you! You hope all this hard work is going to pay off. You watch the eight point come toward you. It's a nice buck, not the big one, but it's a keeper! Just as he gets into shooting range he darts off to chase a doe across the field and they come back toward you to the edge of the woods. He chases her around the field once more to the edge of the woods and the doe stops to rest, and he stops with her. Then, they both look into the woods at the same time. After a few seconds you see the body of a deer step out of the woods. The eight point takes off. You look closer, and IT'S HIM AGAIN! It's the monster! The doe takes off and the monster runs after her. You watch him chase the doe in circles around the field, and then in and out of the woods getting closer each time. Finally, she heads toward you and the monster chases her. You lift your bow and get ready. The doe stops about fifty yards away, and he stops with her. She starts to walk away from you and he follows. You quickly grunt to see if he will stop, and he does! You grunt again. He turns and heads toward you looking like he wants to protect his territory. He gets to forty-five yards, then forty, then thirty-five, and then thirty. He stops and looks away for a second, and you pull back. He walks to twenty-five yards, then twenty. If he would just turn broadside you could get a shot! Just then he starts to walk to your left turning broadside. Here it is. Here's your chance. This is what you've been waiting for, hoping for, praying for, and hunting for. Your knees shake. You can see your breath as you breath quickly, your arm starts to become weak, your at full draw, you take a deep breath, and put your twenty yard pin on the back of his shoulder, and then let it go...TOINK! You watch the arrow make a clean pass through both lungs! YES!! The deer jumps and heads for the other end of the field. You watch him run to the end of the field, and then go down! YES!

I'll never forget that first experience of watching the first deer I ever harvested go down after a kill shot. I can still remember the adrenaline and the emotions that I felt at that moment. I remember just as vividly the emotions I felt right before I shot. I remember hoping I had sighted my bow in well enough to make the kill, praying that I wouldn't flinch on the shot and that my knees would stop shaking, and the helpless feeling of trying to pull the bow back that first time under pressure and wondering if the poundage was set to the max because it felt almost impossible to pull it back! There isn't much time between the harvest coming into kill range and taking the shot, so when that moment arrives we just have to let all the prior preparation and hard work we have done take over and just shoot, and let the results speak for itself! If we have done our part, most likely it will produce a harvest.

In this last secret, which might be just as or more important then the rest, firing your weapon, or obeying and doing what God has put in your heart to do is essential if you're going to experience your spiritual harvest. You can know what your hunting for, scout out your area and set up your stand, get up early and spend all day out in the woods, battle all the elements, take all the risks you want, and even have your weapon sighted in perfectly, but if you don't at least fire the weapon when the opportunity comes to bag your animal you will never experience the harvest and all your hard work will be futile. You can get up early every morning and spend all day with God in your quiet scouted out place, know your Bible from front to back, battle all the elements that life brings, and have great intentions on taking big risks in life when God asks you to, but if you aren't willing to obey and do what He says to do and be what He asks you to be nothing will happen and the satisfaction of harvesting God's full plan for your life will never come.

Now, there are many reasons why we don't fire our weapons or obey. One reason is we get "buck fever," or what we call fear. When we think about what God is calling us to do or be our knees start to shake, our hearts pound fast, and the fear won't let us pull our bow back and shoot or obey. We think of all the reasons why we can't do what God says to do or be. We are afraid we won't have enough finances or provision or that we aren't smart enough or good enough. As I mentioned earlier, when God asked Abraham to leave his family and country to make him the father of many nations Abraham didn't even have a child yet! Imagine the excuses Abraham could have brought to God? He didn't have a child, how was he supposed to be the father of many nations? God told him to go, but didn't tell him where! Abraham definitely had many chances to leave his arrow on his bow and pass up the chance on Gods harvest for his life, but He fired because God told him to. That's the key to your obedience: no matter how it looks or what you think of what God is telling you to do or be, just obey because God told you to. God will always make a way and provide when He is the one that tells you to do it.

One other common reason we don't fire our weapon is because we think sometimes it's not the right shot or the shot is too long, it's a long shot! Sometimes God will ask us to do something or be something and we think we are the long shot, and that there is no way God could use us to do or be what He is asking. We think of our shortcomings or our past failures and we dismiss ourselves of being worthy of what God is calling us to do or be. We see people in the Bible with the same excuse. When God asked Moses to go to Egypt and tell Pharaoh to let the people of God go, Moses came up with many excuses. He told God he didn't think Pharaoh would listen to him, that his speech wasn't eloquent enough to talk, and that he was afraid to because he stuttered! God wasn't interested in Moses shortcomings, He was only interested in His obedience and Moses reluctantly obeyed despite what He thought of himself. When God called Jeremiah to be a prophet Jeremiah's excuse was that he was too young! God wasn't interested in his age because God already knew what Jeremiah could do; He was only interested in his obedience. If God is calling you to do something or be something He will always provide whatever you need when you obey. He would never ask you to do something that would make you look foolish or humiliate you. God knew the plan He had for your life before you were even born.

Another reason why we sometimes don't shoot is because we took that kind of shot before and we missed, so we are afraid to take that shot again! If you've stepped out in faith and obeyed before and you felt you missed it, or it didn't work out, and God is leading you to "shoot" again then do it! How will you know if you will get a harvest if you won't shoot your weapon? Especially if God is leading you to shoot!

God might be asking you to obey in a situation that isn't the best situation to shoot. You know, like a quartering away shot where you shot before and stuck the arrow in the deer's behind! God might be asking you to obey in conditions that aren't perfect where you made a mistake before. If He is then shoot and obey again, and remember if God is leading you to obey then everything will work out to His plan.

What is it that you feel in your heart God is asking you to do as you spend time with Him? What is God asking you to step out in faith to do or be? When "buck fever" sets in and you come up with every excuse why you can't obey what God is saying, just move ahead in faith and let all the preparation and hard work you've already done take over and FIRE YOUR WEAPON at your harvest. Do your part and obey, and leave the results up to God.

YOUR HARVEST

You did it! You got the record book buck! You get on your walkie-talkie and call your friend, and he races to your tree. You climb down and both of you run to your buck. It's massive! You've never seen a rack or a body like it in your life! You hold the buck's head up by the horns and begin to tell your friend how it happened. You stop to enjoy the moment and cherish this moment of fulfillment. You did it!

I remember the night I shot the biggest harvest of my life to date. Although twelve hunting seasons have past since then I still remember almost every detail of that hunt where I harvested a thirteen point that just missed the record books. I remember walking up on that buck and enjoying the fulfillment and happiness I felt at that moment, when I fixed my eyes on the rack and body of that monster. It might sound silly to most, but if you're a true hunter and you've had the experience of bagging a trophy you will understand when I say there aren't many experiences out there like harvesting a big buck.

This next statement also will only be understood by some people who are true hunters of God and have experienced a spiritual harvest that they have hunted with all of their heart for: There is nothing in this world compared to harvesting and living out Gods purpose and plan for your life. What do I mean by a "spiritual harvest?" Your spiritual harvest is the knowing and living out of Gods purpose and plan, but this harvest has many different looks. As you hunt and live out Gods plan you will have times where you see the fulfillment of a dream God has given you, wisdom to know what to do next, answer to prayers you have prayed for many years, the restoration of your health, provision God has given you for a certain need, a restored marriage or relationship, or freedom from an addiction or past hurt. Your harvest could be victory, financial prosperity, or it might be a heavenly reward. Your spiritual harvest could look like many different things, but all spiritual harvest has this in common: It takes a hunt. Remember our definition of hunt at the beginning of the book? Hunt and seek have the same definition. It takes a persistent seeking. It comes out of persistently seeking God and a relationship with Him and leads to fulfillment and happiness in your life. God tells us in Jeremiah 29:13, *"And you will seek Me and find Me, when you search for me with all your heart."* As you hunt God with all your heart you are promised those experiences that compare to no other when you will experience victory, see dreams come to pass, see prayers answered, receive wisdom to know Gods plan, and feel fulfillment in life like you have never felt before that is a million times greater then fixing your eyes on your record book harvest. Harvesting a record book buck is temporary, but spiritual harvest and knowing and living out Gods plan for you is eternal!

Preparation For Your Next Harvest!

You see your buddy stand up and look behind you. "Holy Cow! Look at that!" He says as he points. You look behind you and across the field is another massive buck, and it's even bigger then the one you shot! "No way" you say. At that moment it hits you what the hunt is all about. You think back and remember all the scouting, practicing with your weapon, time put in, battles with the elements, mistakes you've made, risks you've taken, the kill shot you made, and you realize it wasn't just about bagging your trophy buck. It was just as much about preparing you for your next big hunt, because there is always a bigger harvest out there to get! You're satisfied for now, but only until the excitement wears off from the harvest of this buck, and the glimpse of the bigger buck you just saw plays back in your head, and then it starts all over with next years hunt for the next record book buck!

Your harvest isn't just the final outcome or manifestation of something you have hunted for. It's also the process by which you got the harvest. Let's take a look at some basic definitions of the word "harvest" to get an even better idea of what your spiritual harvest is. Encarta World Dictionary defines a harvest as "The consequences of previous actions or behaviors." Merriam-Webster Online Dictionary defines harvest as "an accumulated store or productive result." The American Heritage Dictionary defines the harvest as a "result or consequence of an activity." You see, on your hunt for God and His purpose for your life you will gain something that will prepare you for an even bigger harvest on your next hunt: experience! With your harvest also comes wisdom and knowledge for your next hunt. After you experience harvest you will know the dedication, persistence, determination, and faithfulness it takes to get another! You will understand that it might even mean disappointment, mistakes, sacrifice, and most importantly you will know the depth and intimacy it will take in your relationship with God for you to be fulfilled in life, because you see that's the point of the hunt and is the reason why we are created. Mark 12:30 say, *"And you shall love the Lord your God with all your heart, with all your soul, with all your mind, and with all your strength."* It's not just the harvest that helps you. It is also the process of getting there because God always has an even bigger harvest in store for you! God has a plan and a harvest for your life that is better then you could ever ask for or imagine in your mind! Now every time you get discouraged on your next hunt for your monster harvest you can look back and remember how you got your harvest in the past and be encouraged! It's been a privilege to go on this journey with you! Hopefully this hunting season when you are sitting in your tree stand you will not only hunt the monster harvest of your area, but more importantly the monster harvest God has for your life!

...And now you know the secrets of the hunt! Are you up for the challenge?

CPSIA information can be obtained at www.ICGtesting.com
Printed in the USA
BVOW010623150113

310554BV00008B/131/P